PowerKids Readers:
My World™

My School Bus
A Book About School Bus Safety
Heather Feldman

The Rosen Publishing Group's
PowerKids Press™
New York

For Joshua Max and Jeremy Sherman

Published in 2000 by The Rosen Publishing Group, Inc.
29 East 21st Street, New York, NY 10010

Copyright © 2000 by The Rosen Publishing Group, Inc.

First Edition

Book design: Danielle Primiceri

Photo Illustrations by: Donna M. Scholl

Feldman, Heather L.
     My school bus : a book about school bus safety / by Heather Feldman.
       p.   cm. — (My world)
       Includes index.
       Summary: Photographs and simple text follow a girl on her bus ride to school as she demonstrates the safe way to wait for, board, ride, and leave the bus.
       ISBN 0-8239-5523-0
       1. School children—Transportation—Safety measures—Juvenile literature. 2. School buses—Safety measures—Juvenile literature. [1. School buses—Safety measures. 2. Safety.] I. Title. II. Series: Feldman, Heather L.
My world.
LB2864.F45   1998
372.18'72—dc21

                                       98-31957
                                           CIP
                                          AC

Manufactured in the United States of America

Contents

1 The School Bus   4

2 My Friend Billy   8

3 Words to Know   22

4 Books and Web Sites   23

5 Index   24

6 Word Count   24

7 Note   24

I wait for the yellow school bus every morning. Sometimes my mom waits with me.

When the yellow school bus arrives, the bus driver smiles and says, "Good morning!"

I find my seat right away.
My friend Billy always sits
with me.

Billy and I follow the rules on the bus. We do not stick our hands out the window. We always listen to the bus driver. The rules keep us safe.

11

We always stay in our seats.

We talk quietly.
Sometimes I even tell Billy
a joke.

Sometimes we see what we have for lunch.

When the yellow school bus comes to a stop, we know we can stand up.

19

We walk slowly down
the stairs to school.
Good-bye!

Words to Know

BUS DRIVER   FRIENDS

LUNCH SCHOOL BUS

YELLOW

Here are more books to read about riding the
school bus:
School Bus
by Donald Crews
William Morrow & Co. Inc.

School Bus Driver
by Dee Ready
Capstone Press

To learn more about how to stay safe on a
school bus, check out these Web sites:
http://www.nysgtsc.state.ny.us/kid-schl.htm
http://www.nhsta.dot.gov/kids/bussafety/ind
ex.html

Index

B
bus driver, 6, 10

F
friends, 8

L
lunch, 16

M
morning, 4, 6

R
rules, 10

S
seats, 8, 12
stop, 18

stairs, 20

W
window, 10

Word Count: 107

Note to Librarians, Teachers, and Parents

PowerKids Readers are specially designed to get emergent and beginning readers excited about learning to read. Simple stories and concepts are paired with photographs of real kids in real-life situations. Spirited characters and story lines that kids can relate to help readers respond to written language by linking meaning with their own everyday experiences. Sentences are short and simple, employing a basic vocabulary of sight words, as well as new words that describe familiar things and places. Large type, clean design, and photographs corresponding directly to the text all help children to decipher meaning. Features such as a picture glossary and an index help children get the most out of PowerKids Readers. Lists of related books and Web sites encourage kids to explore other sources and to continue the process of learning. With their engaging stories and vivid photo-illustrations, PowerKids Readers inspire children with the interest and confidence to return to these books again and again. It is this rich and rewarding experience of success with language that gives children the opportunity to develop a love of reading and learning that they will carry with them throughout their lives.